60 Minutes to Success

◆

To my favorite brother —

Happy Lunching!

Rachel & Jeff

60 Minutes to Success

◆

The Ultimate Guide To Power Lunching

Alice A. Adams, Ron Adams, PhD & Rachel A. Seff

Writer's Showcase
presented by *Writer's Digest*
San Jose New York Lincoln Shanghai

60 Minutes to Success
The Ultimate Guide to Power Lunching

Writer's Showcase
presented by *Writer's Digest*
an imprint of iUniverse.com, Inc.

For information address:
iUniverse.com, Inc.
620 North 48th Street, Suite 201
Lincoln, NE 68504-3467
www.iuniverse.com

ISBN: 0-595-13214-6

Printed in the United States of America

Contents

◆

Foreword

◆

Although most adults believe their table manners are reasonably adequate, some job candidates make the mistake of assuming their etiquette is up to par...even when it's not.

And because more corporations are adding a business lunch to their recruitment protocols, more of the nation's top business schools now offer tutoring by etiquette experts before new grads begin their first job searches. The majority, however, do not yet prepare students for conducting successful business lunches and there are, to date, no specific guidelines for job applicants to follow regarding how they should conduct themselves during this portion of the prospective employer's examination.

"60 Minutes to Success: The Ultimate Guide to Power Lunching" not only guides first-time job-seekers through the dizzying maze presented by the business breakfast, lunch, cocktail reception or formal dinner. It also prompts job-changers and corporate managers on how to conduct themselves in interview situations, business lunches or corporate receptions.

A quick read with to-the-point guidance mixed liberally with most-often-asked questions and humorous vignettes, "60 Minutes to Success" combines everything you should have learned in kindergarten with today's corporate expectations in business luncheon situations.

Entertaining-yet-informative, we see "60 Minutes to Success:" as a "must read" for every college graduate, every candidate placement services send on interviews and for every individual who pursues his or her dream job or acceptance into law school, medical school or MBA programs.

Acknowledgements

———————— ◆ ————————

The authors wish to extend their appreciation to everyone who has shared their "business lunch" experiences as information was being compiled for "60 Minutes to Success."

They also are grateful to Kristin Berthelsen for creating the format and for developing the graphic design and for the endless hours she has devoted to the nurture and completion of this project.

Finally, the writers would like to thank the business community for their encouragement and their interest in the development of this book. It is our hope that "60 Minutes to Success" will enhance the success of every recruit and candidate who participates in a business luncheon and, as a result, lands the job of their dreams.

Introduction and History
of the Business Lunch

◆

Introduction and History
of the Business Lunch

◆

History doesn't record the circumstances surrounding the first business lunch. And we don't know the exact date. But we can picture prehistoric cave people gathering to hunt beasts or gather food and taking a rest to share a snack when they became hungry.

Over the past several decades, and particularly after the demise of the two-martini lunch, the business lunch has taken on new dimensions and offers new opportunities and challenges.

Today the business lunch is used to build relationships, to review contracts, to interview job candidates and to ink big deals. A business lunch is always about business. It is rarely about food, nor does it have a total social focus. However, some companies take clients to lunch with the intent of establishing good will.

More corporations now include the business lunch as a part of the interview process. In this setting, the interviewers test a candidate's savvy in a real-time situation and observe a prospective employee's demeanor in a social environment.

It is important to know how the business lunch is usually conducted and what's expected of you—both as a host and as a guest. Bottom line, knowing the seductive art of the successful business lunch can be key to any professional's future.

Unfortunately, many of us are never taught proper table manners in the home, a tradition that has generally gone by the wayside because of dual-income families and parents who are usually just too busy to even sit down to dinner with their children. In the past, these family and special occasion mealtime celebrations were opportunities for children to learn which fork to use, how to eat messy foods without making a mess and how to behave graciously in the company of elders.

It is, indeed, possible for the lack of poise and social grace to short-circuit job offers and for poor table manners to destroy a business relationship.

The purpose of this book is to provide information that is easy to read, easy to access and easy to remember. It has been written for use in preparation for lunch interviews, cocktail receptions and site visits with prospective employers. It also includes pointers for dinner with a prospective manager and his or her spouse or for lunches used to get to know prospective co-workers who may also have some say in the final hiring decision.

This book takes for granted that you are aware of proper business attire for the business lunch and the job interview. And, little space has been devoted here to discuss how to sell yourself and how to answer common questions of an interviewer.

The total focus of this book is on the business meal—how it is conducted, how to present yourself as a savvy professional, how to recover from a *faux pas* and how to be successful in this important social situation.

The priority of this information is to help you prepare to land the job of your life—whether it's the first job after graduation or the job that will eventually propel your career to new heights. Use it as a guide and as a tool to build some essential—and practical—business skills.

Bon appetite!

Power Lunching
in the New Millennium

◆

Power Lunching
in the New Millennium

◆

How powerful are "power lunches?"

Lunch is the "hour of power" in almost every community, from metropolitan areas down to "just a wide spot in the road." Recent mergers and acquisitions and trends toward "rightsizing" have placed a premium on the worker's time. Strategies to keep costs down and productivity up mean business professionals now do some of their "business" in the luncheon setting. This is multi-tasking at its finest—eating and working simultaneously in order to save time!

But be aware of the pitfalls and possible pratfalls when this power lunch becomes a job interview. Eating lunch has always been a social activity and there is a general tendency to just sit back and relax over the lunch hour. Candidates can be easily distracted in this somewhat "laid back" environment. So when you, as a candidate, are in a luncheon interview situation, take care not to fall into the habit of chit-chatting between courses.

Let's go back to the idea of power lunching for a moment. A great story about the late American writer Truman Capote describes how the portly author read through a restaurant's entire menu for what seemed to be a very long time. Finally, he looked up at the waiter, smiled and said with unabashed charm, "I think I'll have…a cookie."

That's power!

So is eating a chef's salad with dressing on the side when everyone else is ordering chicken fried steaks as big as dinner plates and soaked in gravy!

Often, restaurant reviewers today classify restaurants as being "good power-lunching restaurants" where commerce and cuisine blend easily and conversations about surviving "the jungle out there" flow from one table to the next.

It's also interesting that we *eat* breakfast and we *have* dinner…but we "do" lunch, much like we "do" the laundry, the yard work or taxes. Similarly, business lunches are often as much fun as a sharp stick in the eye but we continue to "do" them, nonetheless.

We encourage you to think of the business lunch as having three specific components: a beginning (meeting and greeting), a middle (wining and dining) and an end (win that promotion, make that sale or get that job!)

Making the Appointment for the Business Lunch

◆

Making the Appointment for the Business Lunch

◆

Who Makes the Decision of Where to Eat?

Normally, the person inviting you will select the restaurant or place for lunch. However, they may sometimes ask you where you would like to dine. In some cases, they may ask about any dietary restrictions.

Be ready with answers to any of these questions and have a favorite restaurant in mind, should they ask for recommendations.

Remember, too, that recruiters and interviewers generally schedule many luncheon interviews throughout the fall and spring recruiting season, so it's a nice change of pace for them when a candidate can suggest a new, trendy place to eat.

Answer These Questions
Before Meeting the Recruiter For Lunch

* What is this lunch supposed to accomplish?
* Are there any parking arrangements/specific directions?
* Who will be interviewing me?
* How much time should I allot for the interview?
* Where will I be meeting my interviewer?

* Are there forms to be filled out before the interview?
* Anything special I should bring to the interview?

Two recruiters invited an applicant to lunch just before the Christmas holidays. This individual not only came highly recommended but also had a stellar resume. After the usual conversational amenities, the trio spoke about the company and one recruiter described the job opening in specifics.

The candidate seemed to be drinking in every detail. Then the second recruiter leaned forward, wanting to give the applicant an opportunity to talk about how he would fit into the corporate culture. "Tell us, Rob. Just what can you bring to this party?" The applicant thought a moment and then tried to answer humorously, "How about chips and dips?" The joke fell flat and needless to say, he didn't get the job.

If the recruiter asks you to bring materials with you, such as a copy of your transcript or a list of references, you should keep these items in a briefcase or a portfolio. If you do not own these items, a plain manila folder will work just as well, and it can be kept on the floor beneath your seat while you lunch.

How To Meet a Stranger

It probably isn't necessary to wear a white rose in your lapel when meeting someone you've never met before. Just give Mr. Smith a good description of yourself and ask him to describe himself—height, weight, etc. Then make certain you are on time and you are where you've said you will be.

In most restaurants, the host or hostess will seat you in a waiting area or at the bar and you can instruct them you are awaiting the arrival of Mr. or Ms. Smith with ABC Company. When your party arrives, they will usher them to you.

Or more preferably, you should simply ask the host or hostess whether or not they suggest you remain standing in the foyer or should be seated at a table. Most recruiters have good relationships with their favorite restaurants, and often the host will know what the recruiters prefer.

How To Choose The Restaurant…
If They Ask You to Choose

If it is left to you to choose the restaurant for a business lunch, always select a restaurant where you've dined several times before. Think of the quality of the meal. Think, also, of the atmosphere—Is it too loud to hear conversation? Is service prompt and not disruptive? Is there something for every taste, including vegetarians or those on low-fat or low-calorie diets?

Secondly, the word to remember is "location, location, location!" The restaurant you choose should be fairly central and easy to find with ample parking spaces.

Need a little help. Try the internet. There are lots of websites that feature restaurants like CitySearch.com or OpenTable.com. Using these websites will help you with location, cuisine, and maybe even price. So with just a click of a button, you can choose a restaurant and make reservations. You may also want to make special requests like away from high traffic zones, the kitchen, or the restrooms. This will ensure that you will have a suitable environment for your business lunch.

Emergency Back-ups
(Extra Tie, Make-up, Spare Stockings, etc.)

Rule one is a no-brainer: Keep an umbrella in your car in case of rain.

Keep an emergency repair kit in your glove box. It should contain the following: a pin-on replacement button as well as a small sewing kit if you lose or break a button en route; double-sided cellophane tape—in case a skirt or trouser hem unravels before you arrive. Just tape it back into place until you can sew it later. Also keep an extra comb, tooth-brush and travel-size toothpaste, hair spray, aspirin and breath mints. (Women may also want to keep face powder, blush and lipstick plus an extra pair of pantyhose in the emergency kit, just in case those you are wearing develop a surprise run.)

Professional Business Attire The Rule... Even on Casual Fridays

Your goal is to make an outstanding first impression, right?

So men should stick to dark colors, such as navy, gray or black. A pressed white shirt and a great power tie are important. Select black or cordovan shoes and black socks. Be clean-shaven (no goatees or longer sideburns, please). And have a short, fashionably styled haircut.

Women should wear dark, jewel-tone colors, such as blue, black, emerald, burgundy or beige. The younger you are, the longer your skirt should be. Remember, Ali McBeal may be a great lawyer, but her suits would never pass muster in an interview. Select sheer pantyhose, mini-mal jewelry and an appropriate scarf or pin. Wear a natural-look make-up and pull long hair out of your face (there's nothing more distracting than someone—male or female constantly brushing their hair behind an ear or out of their face.)

Save dousing in perfume or after-shave for an evening out. Just plain soap and deodorant will suffice. Some interviewers may be allergic to your favorite fragrance.

Take keys and other spare change out of your pockets. No one wants to be remembered as the applicant who jingled when they walked.

How Long Should a Business Lunch Last?

No longer than 60 minutes. Some will stretch into 90 minutes, allow-ing for travel within this time period.

Meeting, Greeting and Seating

◆

Meeting, Greeting and Seating

◆

How you meet and greet others creates a lasting impression—for good or evil. If you are easy to meet and know how to greet strangers, you are almost always assured of a positive encounter.

It may sound too simplistic, but your ability to handle business lunch situations—from greetings and introductory handshakes to saying good-bye and your note of thanks—can make a difference in the speed of your rising star.

Your Arrival

If you are the host, arrive 10-15 minutes ahead of time to make sure each guest is welcomed and made to feel at ease.

If you are the guest, it goes without saying. BE ON TIME—or even a few minutes early.

If you are the first to arrive, do not be seated. Give the restaurant host your name and who you are waiting for and then take a seat, facing the door to watch for your host's arrival.

When the host arrives, they most likely indicate where you should sit—or you can just ask, "Where would you like for me to sit?"

If you're wearing a hat and coat and no one directs you to a place to put them, simply ask, "Where should I hang my coat?" This situation is more likely to occur in colder climates—coats are no big thing in the South or on the West Coast.

The Business Greeting

Shaking Hands: Signaling the Beginning of the Relationship

Handshakes are important—and how often are we reminded to offer a firm, sincere grip? And just as important as the handshake—is eye contact.

But remember this—if you crush someone's hand in a handshake, you may be setting a negative tone—like you're attempting to be some kind of control freak. Or, if the person is suffering from arthritis or other tendon or joint problems, a mighty handshake may just send them into orbit with pain.

It is also inappropriate grasp the other person's elbow when shaking hands or to pump the person's arm up and down like you would at an old-fashioned gas station. Just a relaxed grip, good eye contact, a smile and a, "It is good to meet you," will do.

If someone doesn't extend a hand to shake on first meeting, withdraw your hand. Then smile and say, "It's so nice to meet you."

Women should practice their handshake on a friendly male partner, to make sure they don't have the Princess Di grip, one in which just the fingers are extended in a dainty fashion instead of the whole hand.

In a good handshake, whether done between same sex partners or the opposite sex, both hands should come firmly together and have an equal grip.

The first part of the lunch (the greeting) should begin with a few minutes of small talk. This builds the relationship and puts both parties at ease. No good at small talk? Then, make sure you read the local newspaper that morning so you can talk about the weather or local sports teams. It's also a good idea to watch the local and national news the night before to make sure you're up on current events.

Keep your conversation upbeat and positive. Do not talk about the traffic problems in the city. No one wants to dine with a complainer. After ordering your food, launch into your business discussion because no one wants to talk actual business when they are eating.

When in Rome...or France....

It is not uncommon that some business associates will hug or kiss when they greet each other. At the risk of sounding ultra-conservative, our opinion is to confine greeting gestures to a handshake. If you have long-standing business relationships, hugging may be comfortable, but kissing may create discomfort for others in the group.

If someone kisses you hello, unexpectedly, try not to react negatively—but if you have the opportunity later on, when you are alone with this person, you may want to say, "You really caught me off guard. I don't usually greet business associates in that way." This gives the gentle message that you'd prefer a handshake.

Interviewees should be particularly aware of cultural differences. If you are interviewing with a multinational Japanese company, remember to bow your head slightly as you shake hands.

French and Lebanese corporate employees almost always give the 'double-sided kiss-kiss' when they greet one another.

Cultural differences can be a sticky issue. When in doubt, consult the recruiter for the company and ask what greeting is preferred.

Handling Business Introductions

◆

Handling Business Introductions

◆

Your ability to handle business introductions is a skill that should be perfected before inserting yourself in any interview situation. It is important to be savvy in this area. If you're not, memorize these three rules:

(1) Always say the name of the person you are introducing "to." Say, *John Jones, I'd like *to* introduce Jane Smith." Or, "John Jones, may I introduce Jane Smith."

(2) Always introduce a younger person *to* an older person. Mr. Jones, may I introduce my classmate Jerry Jenkins?"

(3) A lesser rank is always introduced to a higher rank. Mr. Jones (CEO), may I introduce Mark Wallace, a student at the University. Or, you may say, John Jones, I'd like to introduce our new office manager, Jane Smith.

(*A footnote. Use first names only if it is the culture of the organization. Otherwise, say, "Mr. Jones, may I introduce Mrs. Smith?" And one more thing: when introducing anyone, clarify their relationship to you—it could save questions later.) It is always better to err on the side of conservatism.

As you introduce someone, look at them. By doing so, you draw attention to them and make them feel important at the same time.

At a business meal, always introduce yourself to the people around you and offer business cards. When introducing yourself, use both names. "Hi, I'm John Jones." It conveys you are an adult and not stuck eternally in your high school or college fraternity persona.

If you have forgotten someone's name because introductions usually come in groups and are rapid-fire, simply say, "I'm sorry. I've forgotten your name" or, "I remember you are an alum at the university but your name has slipped my mind."

Introductions are an emotional part of any meeting. No business professional would admit to this, but it is undoubtedly the case.

Remembering one introduction, a now-CEO recalls how disgusted he was with his boss when he was introduced this way. "Oh, and this is Charlie. He's an important part of our team—whenever he's awake." Old Charlie wasn't outwardly offended by this "tribute" but he remembered it, even 10 years after the event.

If you are in charge of introductions, after naming the person— mention something they do. For example, say "Mr. Jones, I'd like you to meet Alicia Holmes. Alicia is president of our Young Business Leaders Association, and she's also a Cowboys fan, something I believe you two have in common."

By providing some additional information, you serve each of the people you introduce with a plateful of conversational possibilities. And, once you've made the introductions, you may stay and talk about the Cowboys or move on, leaving Mr. Jones and Alicia Holmes to discuss topics of current interest or whatever is appropriate, depending on the win-loss totals.

For what it's worth: During a site-visit by college recruits to a large corporation, the chief executive officer dropped by a table at lunch in one of the company's meeting rooms. Later, the CEO instructed the recruiter conducting the discussion, "Don't issue job offers to any of them. If they're not polished enough to stand when I approach their table, they're not the caliber of people we need."

What About Seating?

How people are seated at a business lunch can make a big difference, not only the conversation, but in the outcome of the meeting.

As mentioned earlier, don't just sit down if you are a guest. Ask the host where he wants you to sit. If you are a host, direct each guest to his or her seat. Having a pre-arranged seat will make guests feel important because you've taken the time to plan the seating arrangement.

If you are sitting at the table with two other associates, try to sit with one person across from you and one person to your left. This way, you can address both individuals at once. Job candidates sitting in the middle of two interviewers always wind up feeling as though they were watching a tennis match.

When To Present Your Business Card

First decide if you need a business card—and, without question, the answer should be "yes!" In fact, we recommend "generic" business cards from the time you enter college as a first-year student. These cards should be simple: Name, mailing address, telephone and e-mail address.

> Ima Verygood Candidate
> 123 Main Street, Apt. 456
> Houston, Texas 77123
> (713) 555-1234 (H)
> (713) 777-6789 (W)
> *ImaCandidate@Hiremetodayplease.com*

One rule of thumb is that the person of higher rank should request a card. Decide how the luncheon goes before presenting a card to everyone. (Remember this—the people you don't want to hear from are probably the ones who will use your business card the most).

Present your business card at the end of the meal—on request or if you think there may be reason for further conversation. Presenting a business card as people leave makes it easier for them to reach their card cases or wallets and can file your card before lunch is served.

Passing out business cards to everyone—like passing out fliers at the mall—only guarantees that few will use them. Be selective, but take advantage of ripe opportunities.

A Word About Electronic Communications

All professionals understand the importance of being accessible and being electronically up-to-date. However, if you are interviewing for a job and are asked to participate in a business lunch, leave your cell phone and your pager at home or in the car.

Very few circumstances are more important than making your best impression and focusing on the conversations taking place. Someone getting calls at the table or constantly checking their pagers for messages may appear obnoxious or at the very least, distracted—and possibly not interested. Before an interview, turn off your cellular phone or leave it in your car...and NEVER speak on a cell phone at the table!

Who Orders First and Other Social Sequences

◆

Who Orders First
—and Other Social Sequences

◆

Generally, the host orders first—and may offer to order for the rest of the table. However, if the host asks you to order for yourself, quickly make your selection so you won't hold up the process.

Under no circumstances should you order anything while waiting for others of your luncheon party to arrive. It shows you don't have the patience or the courtesy to wait.

Being prepared and efficient at the luncheon table speaks worlds about how organized you are and how well you understand the value of time.

Which Napkin—and Other Nifty Napkin Info

As soon as everyone is seated, the host places the napkin in his or her lap to signal the start of the meal. Napkins are generally located on the left of your plate, or sometimes directly on your plate.

Napkins can be a challenge but usually are helpful in keeping your manners on the straight and narrow. Napkins come in handy if you end up with food on your face or your clothing. Napkins are also a good way to keep your mouth dry after drinking.

Don't rub anything with your napkin. A napkin's sole purpose in life is to blot. A napkin is never used to blow one's nose or to wipe sweat from the forehead.

Most people don't usually place their napkins in their laps until they are ready to eat, but if your table is going to have a drink before the meal, place the napkin in your lap as soon as everyone at the table is seated.

If you are called away from the table, take your napkin and place it in your chair. Never put a used napkin on the table—it's just so unhygienic.

If your napkin falls on the floor, just like a lost eating utensil, ask the waiter to be kind enough to bring you another.

For what it's worth: A candidate from a college in the northeast came to Texas for a job interview. During dinner at a Mexican restaurant, hot tortillas were brought in a round, insulated container. At the end of the meal, no one had opened the tortillas, so the candidate did so out of curiosity. When she opened the container, she mistook the tortillas for the hot hand towels that were often provided in the Asian restaurants where she had grown up, so she delicately took one of the still-warm tortillas (which are meant to be eaten with chicken and beef Fajitas), patted her mouth and wiped her hands.

What To Do With Those Empty Sweetener Packets ???

No matter where you dine or what you eat, there are usually wrappings to contend with. They may be as small as an empty sugar or sweetener package. And they may be as bulky as a miniature butter tub with a zip-off top. In general, the best way to dispose of these empty wrappings is to crumple them and put them to the side of the plate. This is perfectly acceptable. DO NOT PUT THEM IN YOUR POCKET!

How To Squeeze Lemon Slices Without Making a Splash

No biggie. While squeezing a lemon wedge into iced tea or over fish, just unobtrusively cover it with your other hand so it doesn't spritz the rest of the table.

Seasonings and Condiments

With salt on the list of heart-healthy no-no's, it is often seen as bad form to vigorously salt and pepper any items from the menu. Manners mavens and others suggest that it is first advisable to taste the dish before covering it with salt, pepper or sauce of any description—and that includes catsup.

But here's another "seasonings" story you may want to remember:

> *A gentlemen interviewing for a position with IBM was taken out to eat with a group of IBMers. Later, one of the men took him aside and told him he had passed the "big" test with the head man. The test had to do with the salt and pepper shakers on the table. "If you had automatically seasoned your steak and potato before tasting it, you wouldn't have a chance for the job…because the head man strongly believes that if you did not think about every detail, you wouldn't perform this job well at all."*

The Right Stuff—
What You Need to Know About Alcohol

First of all, there is nothing written that says you have to order an alcoholic beverage at a business lunch. For simplicity's sake, we recommend ordering tea or coffee, cola or bottled water.

The second part of the unwritten rule about business and alcohol is—if you drink, don't overindulge. Too often people see the business lunch as an opportunity for free food and drink. This should not be your focus. You are here to accomplish an important goal—to sell your-self to a prospective employer. Stay sober so you'll be in control of your-self—and possibly future opportunities and relationships.

However, if someone tries to insist you join them in a glass of wine or sings the praises of this restaurant's Margaritas, don't get hyper and respond, "Oh no. I don't drink!" Just say, "A glass of tea will be fine right now."

If a female host orders beer and the waiter pours the first glass, when that glass is empty, it is the host's responsibility to refill the glass. You may ask if you may pour it for her—but give her time to refill the glass before you offer.

If champagne is being served and you don't care for champagne, don't make it a big deal by taking your champagne flute and turning it upside down. Just allow the champagne to be poured and then hold your water glass when toasts are being made.

When Wine is Served

The whole wine ceremony may seem intimidating, but it really isn't. It's not a taste test to see whether you like a wine but to find out whether the wine has been stored properly and if it has spoiled.

After making a selection, be sure and check the label when the server brings it to your table. You will want to assure if it's a '92 on the menu that they don't bring a '94 instead.

You should look at the wine in the glass, smell it and taste it. If it's bad, you'll know immediately and they should offer to bring a replacement.

Then, there's the question of whether you should drink at all. If you're on a job interview and trying to impress someone, remember that alcohol loosens the tongue. It's probably best to order bottled water or an ice tea.

What To Do If You Spill Your Water?

Let's face it. We're all fallible human beings. Sooner or later, we're going to spill the water, drag a sleeve through the gravy or send food careening off our plates when cutting tough meat.

The point of this topic is what to do when it happens. So, here are some rules—not hard and fast—but practical reactions to "situations."

When you spill your water, the first thing is to right the glass or cup. The second inclination is to begin madly sopping water with your napkin. But don't! Instead, apologize for the inconvenience and excuse yourself. Find a waiter and explain the situation. Then return to the table and stand by until the waiter has sponged up the water, replaced watery plates and brought new silverware.

Some may be prone to say something clever, but if 'clever' is not your nature, apologize again, say nothing about the incident and carry on with other conversation. DON'T DWELL ON YOUR CLUMSINESS.

If the server comes by to refill water or beverages and you prefer no refills, simply say, "No thank you." There's no need to put your napkin or your hand over the glass so it can't be refilled.

For what it's worth: One applicant had the misfortune of spilling pea soup on the white collar of her black interview suit at the beginning of a lunch interview. Unfortunately she did not notice the pea soup stain until she excused herself to the powder room at the end of the meal.

Horrified that her luncheon companions did not bring the spill to her attention, she timidly returned to the table and graciously asked the waiter to bring some seltzer water (famous for removing stains).

The moral of this story: We're all human and everyone experiences these horrifying situations. Take it in stride—and never let them see you sweat!

What About Trips to the Men's/Women's Room?

If you need to leave the table in the middle of the meal, fold your napkin and leave it on your chair and graciously excuse yourself.

When Asked a Question
and You Have a Mouthful of Food?

Either motion for them to wait until you've finished chewing or, if possible, say, "Just a moment, please." Then, take your time. If you rush, you may end up gagging or spewing food over your tablemates. Neither is appetizing. This situation ultimately underscores a good reason for taking small bites, so try to order food that is able to be cut into smaller, bit-sized pieces.

Chicken and fish are always safe bets. Beef takes a little longer to chew. If you desire pasta, choose a penne pasta or one that is served in smaller pieces.

What If You Find a Bone in Your Orange Juice?

Barry L. O'Donnell, associate MBA director at Virginia Tech in Blacksburg, VA well remembers this story from his days in HR with NationsBank: "One of our candidates was having breakfast with a bank employee who had attended the same university. During the meal, just as she was taking a drink of juice, the candidate got a funny look on her face and peered into the glass. The glass of juice, it seems, had been served containing a rather large chicken bone. She handled the situation well, bringing it to the attention of her dining partner and the waiter. We never figured this one out, but the hotel didn't bill us for her stay."

Appetizers

---◆---

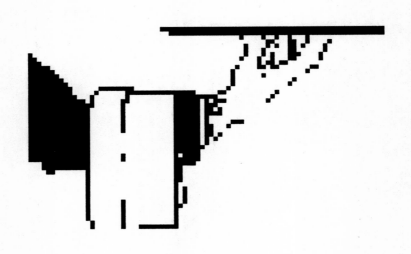

Appetizers

---◆---

What Comes First—Ordering, Business or Chit-chat?

After everyone is seated, spend a few minutes in chit-chat while looking over the menu. Then order and continue the chat for a few moments before ratcheting over to the business of the day. It's perfectly permissible to talk about sports, the weather, this great city, etc., in the interim. Talk about the restaurant or anything that could be of interest to your dining partners.

The time to discuss business is after the appetizer is served. Never wait until dessert to begin discussing your 10-point list of priorities.

If there are papers or graphics to be reviewed, do this before the entrée or after lunch during coffee—if the opportunity arises.

If you want to take notes on what is discussed, be aware—it is difficult to focus on the conversation, take notes and eat at the same time. Because business lunches are usually brief (sometimes an hour or less), it may be best to leave your pen and paper in your car. Then, at the end of the meal—after all the "good-byes" have been said, jot down points to remember.

Do You Order Appetizers For the Table If You're Hosting?

Yes! But make sure you ask your table what they would prefer. Some may have dietary restrictions.

The 'Fork Thing'

As incredible as it sounds, many people get 'up tight' when they see more than one or two forks in a table setting. We say "incredible" because most people know how to do tasks that are much more complex—like run computers, build buildings, figure complicated tax returns, etc.

So what's so bad about not being up on the 'fork thing?'

At the very worst, you run out of forks at the end of the meal and have to ask the waiter for a dessert fork. At the very best, the number of utensils at your plate.

Here's the deal: When it comes to forks, use the one on the left, and then work your way from the outside in. That's all. It's that simple!

The one fork that isn't on the left is the one resting on the big soup spoon—to the right of the knives that are next to the plate. You'll see this small fork only when you are going to be eating oysters.

Use the big spoon for soup.

Most establishments serve two forks—the outer for salad and the larger one for the entrée.

To the left of the plate are the forks. The one closest to the plate is for salad and cheese. The next is for meat. If fish is being served, sometimes a third fork is added.

You may sometimes see three knives lined up at the right side of the plate—the most inward for salad and cheese, the middle for cutting meat and the most outer, a butter knife.

A dessert fork will be brought with dessert, and will sometimes be accompanied by a spoon.

Joy Miller, Coordinator of Experiential Education at Thiel College in Greenville, PA, tells this story about forks: A dinner meeting was held, bringing together a job candidate with a team of recruiters. During the salad course, the candidate lost her grip and dropped her salad fork, which landed in one of the recruiter's lap...where it stayed for the entire meal.

What should she have done? Apologize for the slip and ask the waiter for a replacement utensil.

Enjoy Your Lunch...Acceptably

◆

Enjoy Your Lunch...Acceptably

◆

How To Enjoy Your Soup Without Being Offensive

Although they seem fairly non-threatening, soups often present problems for the average business lunch. Some are served cold—like gazpachos. Some are served hot. Some have huge chunks of meat and vegetables. Others are thick and creamy.

The socially accepted way of eating soup is to use a soup spoon and always spoon soup *away* from you and toward the center of the bowl. At the last mouthfuls, it is perfectly polite to tilt the bowl away from you.

The soup spoon should be held parallel to the mouth and the soup should be poured from the spoon into the mouth. The only exception would be if you were eating pieces of vegetables or meat—at which point, they would be eaten from the front of the spoon. NO SLURPING, PLEASE!

If the soup is obviously hot, it is permissible to lightly blow on the spoonful before putting it into your mouth, but don't be obvious as you cool each bite.

If the soup is served in a cup with one or two handles, it is permissible to drink from the cup but probably more practical to eat the mushrooms, meatballs or noodles in the soup before drinking the broth.

When you have finished the soup course, leave the spoon in the soup plate or beside the cup.

The Art of Serving Salad and Other Little Known Crudites

Salads are usually served in individual portions on individual plates. However, if the salad comes in a large bowl—"family style"—the correct way to serve it is to use both the salad spoon and the fork in one hand. The salad plate or bowl should be half-filled.

The salad plate, by the way, will always be placed either in the middle of the serving plate or on the left of the luncheon/dinner plate. The bread and butter plate is usually placed in the upper right-hand quadrant of the setting.

Slicing Cherry Tomatoes Without 'Seeding' Tablemates

Cherry tomatoes always seem to present a challenge, for some reason. But, if you like cherry tomatoes, take heart. It is possible to eat a cherry tomato without sending seeds spraying across the table.

By using your knife to steady it, simply pierce the tomato with a salad fork to hold it while cutting. Use the knife to cut it in half and then into quarters, if it is large enough to do this without macerating it.

Never put a whole cherry tomato into your mouth at one time.

The Naked Salad—How To Put On The Dressing

Usually, dressing is brought in a gravy-style dish and served with a side spoon. Do not pour the dressing onto your salad. Instead, spoon the dressing out and then pass it to your neighbor on your left.

Have Your Bread and Butter It, Too...The Right Way

When you are offered a basket of rolls, take one roll and put it on your bread plate. Then break off a small piece. Use the little butter fork (not your own butter knife) to transfer a small bit of butter from the community plate to your own bread plate. Butter your own piece of bread with your own knife and eat it. NEVER use your roll as a "pusher" or to sop gravy at the end of the meal.

Always break your bread and return it to your bread plate. Your butter knife stays on this plate throughout the meal.

Chef's Pick of the Day

◆

Chef's Pick of the Day

◆

Entrees to Avoid During a Business Lunch

While studying the menu, don't be afraid to ask the server how something is prepared or to let them know if you have specific needs. Specifically, avoid:

Anything you'd normally eat with your fingers, like fried chicken.

Sandwiches that are larger than a comfortable mouthful. We stay away from burgers, club sandwiches and deli sandwiches stuffed with pastrami.

Anything smothered with gooey, greasy sauce. It's always the case—if you order something with greasy sauce, it usually falls on your clothing in the spot most obvious for the rest of the day.

Long stringy pasta, like spaghetti.

Anything you can't pronounce.

Anything you've never eaten before.

Anything that drips.

Also avoid anything with gobs of garlic or onion, particularly if you have to go back to the company that afternoon for another session of interviews.

The most expensive entrée on the menu. Stay conservative.

If you know enough about your host to know she or he is health-conscious, it would serve you well to order something on the healthy side of the menu, like broiled fish or chicken—or a large chef salad, perhaps.

Back To the Basics

Your parents were right. Table manners are very important, especially at lunches where companies are considering you for a possible job.

Here are a few "don'ts." Engrave them on your brain.

DON'T...

Eat rapidly or take large bites. Small ones are better and more easily digested (Choking on food at the table is embarrassing and sometimes fatal—unless a nearby diner knows the Heimlich Maneuver).

Don't cut a roll or other breads with your knife. Break them with your hands and butter each bite before eating. Once you begin eating the bread, don't butter it.

Don't push your plate away from you to signal you're through with your meal. Place knife and fork together with knife blade pointed toward the center of the plate and handles resting on the rim.

Don't ask for a doggie bag—EVER.

Don't slump. Sit up straight. Take your elbows off the table. (It is only permissible to place your elbows on the table between courses, not when you are eating.

Don't salt and pepper your order until you've taken a bite or two.

Don't reach. If you need a condiment (like catsup or salad dressing), ask, "After you've used the salad dressing, would you please pass it to me?"

Don't chew with your mouth open or talk while your mouth is full.

Don't forget your napkin. Use it to blot your lips before drinking (this keeps food off the side of your glass).

Don't put food you've dropped back on the plate. If food falls off your plate, pick it up with silverware and put it to the side.

Don't dive for a fallen utensil. If you drop a knife, fork or spoon on the floor, pick it up only if it is reachable. If it is not, ask for the server's assistance. Don't hunt around under the table. In both cases, the server will have to replace it with a clean one.

Don't wander. Only leave the table for emergency purposes.

Being Prepared: Ten Interview Questions That You Should Answer

◆

Being Prepared: Ten Interview Questions That You Should Answer

◆

Describe yourself.

What are your strengths and weakness?

What qualifications do you have that would make you a success in this position?

What are your long and short term goals and what are your steps to meeting those goals?

How well do you work under pressure? Describe the way you would handle a tight deadline.

How would you carry out a project from start to finish?

How do you evaluate success? How would you define working too hard?

In a team situation, are you a leader, a player, an enthusiast, or a motivator?

When you are starting a new job, how would you gain the respect of your coworkers in a month, two months, and three months?

What qualities does a successful manager posses? Describe how you would work under a demanding manager.

Good Table Conversation

Good Table Conversation

◆

> "The mark of a good conversationalist is how well they pay attention to what people say."
> —**Larry King**

There's also an old adage that goes something like, "We were given two ears and only one mouth so we will spend twice as much time listening as talking."

It's true. Spend twice as much time listening as talking. If you are doing all the talking, there's something wrong with this picture. Silence is okay.

Don't force the conversation. If nobody's talking, bring up common knowledge topics—like something you like about the restaurant or what you've heard about the great food, etc.

An "open-ended question" usually is one that must be answered by more than one word. You can sometimes generate conversation by asking open-ended questions beginning with who, what, when, where and why?

Generally, none of us handle pauses in the conversation very well. If it happens over lunch, take a long sip of your water, thoughtfully butter your bread or add sweetener to your coffee or tea and stir slowly.

If there's a lull in the conversation, it is up to the host to keep it going. If you happen to be the host, come prepared with current events, headlines from this morning's newspaper or last night's sports scores. Otherwise, keep quiet and give the people you meet room to talk about themselves. Most people appreciate the opportunity…and you can learn a lot in the process.

And when speaking to anyone, remember we all like our space. In a room full of strangers, it is important to stay between three and five feet away. Asians often stand farther apart. People from Mediterranean and Latin American countries often stand closer than the American standard.

Getting Down To Business—Making The Transition Between Small-Talk and Business

If the host leaves it up to you, simply say how much you appreciate the opportunity to learn more about ABC Company and that you have a few questions (you've done your homework and prepared).

There's one truism of every business person around the world—they like nothing better than to talk about their business. By asking questions, you give them a chance to tell you about their business and they can, in turn, ask some questions of you.

It may be that the host purposely did not begin the business portion of the meal to see if you were savvy enough to take charge of the direction of the conversation.

If the host persists in small talk—about his or her Saturday golf game or exploits with the soccer team—wait until they are through talking before you begin asking your prepared questions.

Staying On Task—How Important Is It?

Very!

You came to this lunch with a purpose. So did your host. Make certain there is as much time as possible for both of you to meet your goals. Small talk at the beginning of the lunch serves to break the ice for conversations later that may include opportunities for you at this company, what you expect to achieve during your tenure with this company and the rewards that are possible.

Topics You Should Avoid

It's a long-standing cliché—never talk about politics or religions at a business lunch or social event. But there are a few more items to avoid as well:

(1) Never engage in gossip—about anyone.

(2) Never badmouth a former boss or employer.

(3) Never go on and on about kids or dogs—bor-r-r-r-ing!

(4) Always respond to questions about your family and lifestyle but never initiate this topic on your own.

Coffee and Dessert

◆

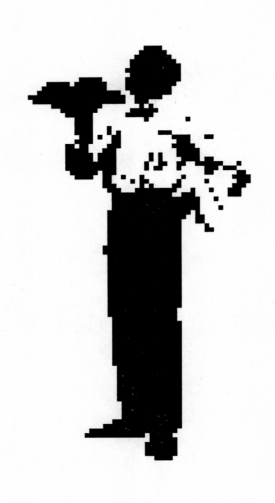

Coffee and Dessert

◆

How to Handle Dessert

This may be too simple. Don't order dessert unless others do first. Your host may be on a tight schedule and your additional order could require an additional 15 minutes.

If the host asks if you would like dessert, it is perfectly acceptable to partake. However, sharing servings or "bites" with other diners during a business lunch should be avoided.

When To Order Coffee After a Meal

See above.

Check, Please!

◆

Check, Please!

◆

Who Pays?

Without question, and in most situations, the person inviting you to lunch will pay. However, if they do not, go to the lunch with money or credit card if everyone is expected to pay for their own meal. (This would be a unique situation, though.)

If you are having lunch because a recruiter or a business person says something like, "We ought to get together for lunch next week," then you should be prepared to pay at least your part of the tab for this informal situation.

The only situations where you obviously are not expected to pay is when the host makes it clear you are coming as a corporate guest—or if the lunch takes place in a private club.

How To Ask For The Check—And When?

If you are the host, check to see if all members of your party have completed their meals. To signal that you have finished eating, place your folk and your knife parallel with the ends resting on the center of the plate and the handles balanced on the plate's rim.

If the tab is brought to the table, leave it face down on the table until the end of the meal. Then, if you usually check the tab to make certain everything ordered is properly priced, there is nothing wrong with using a calculator, but do it discreetly—no mumbling as you add, subtract and carry.

If you are paying the tab, make arrangements with the restaurant head of time to pick it up when you are walking out. If possible, try to avoid having the tab brought to the table.

Tips on Tipping, Etc.

"Gratuity" means giving something "beyond obligation" for a service, a tradition that dates back to the year 1540. The word "tip" has been around since 1755 and was initially defined as "a gift or money given for a service performed." TIP translates: To Insure Promptness.

If you are hosting and are paying the tab, be discreet about the tip. Don't say something like, "The service was lousy. How does he expect me to tip him 15 percent?" Simply add 15 percent to your tab and be done with it.

In many states a tip of 15 percent is easy to figure out because the tax rate is 8.25 percent. So to figure your tip, simply double your tax!

Fifteen percent is the standard tip and should be adequate in most situations—except when the service charge has already been added to the tab. In four-star restaurants, the tip should be 20 percent of the tab.

How to End
the Business Lunch Meeting

◆

How to End
the Business Lunch Meeting

———————— ◆ ————————

Wait and let your host make the first move to end the meeting.

However, if you have a tight schedule and need to leave at the end of an hour, wind the conversation down like this: (1) Summarize the conversation. (2) If you are interested in pursuing the job, now that you have more information, let the host know this. Ask if there is any more documentation needed to make their decision. (3) Thank your host for the opportunity to learn more about the company. Also thank him or her for the delicious lunch and the time they've spent with you. (4) Stand to signal your intentions about ending the meeting. (5) Shake hands warmly, smile and make eye contact. (6) Walk out together unless the host would like to refresh in the restroom. In this case, bid him or her farewell. Thank them again for the lunch and leave. (7) Write a thank-you letter, emphasizing the main points you want them to remember and thanking him or her again for lunch.

How You Know Lunch Was A Success?

Sounds like a question with the obvious answer, "When they offer you the job." But this isn't always true.

For some reason, you may not be the right person for THIS PARTIC-ULAR job, but making a good impression may open other doors down the line.

Sometimes you never know whether lunch was a success or not—unless, of course, you get the offer.

Our advice is go with a purpose—to get to know management, to sell yourself, to let them know about additional experience or skills that make you the right person for the job. And, don't forget this—some recruiters "do lunch" to see how you fit socially, to see how well you meet new people, how well you converse in a strange situation with strange people.

A Few Situations To Avoid…At All Costs

Smoking. Just don't do it. If you're a smoker, wait until you get home to enjoy that cigarette.

Don't chew gum or suck on mints.

Avoid gossip about anyone, anywhere, for any reason.

Avoid drinking too much. This means two drinks…or less.

Don't talk about your diet, how you once weighed 300 pounds and lost 100. And, at all costs, don't remark about anyone's size (if they're thin, they may be anorexic. If they're fat, they may be the manager's wife or a close relative).

Keep the "fat jokes" to yourself. The same goes for ethnic and religious jokes and those with sexual innuendo.

Close each conversation. Don't leave someone hanging because you see someone across the room you want to talk to.

Don't be critical of your school, a particular professor, a previous employer or your parents.

NEVER say anything negative about another member of the corporate community—especially another company who may be recruiting you.

No controversial subjects, please.

Avoid terms like "old" as in "old woman" or "old man." The acceptable term is "senior" or "senior citizen." And "woman" is the opposite of "man." Women over age 18 prefer "woman" to "girl," just as men over age 18 prefer "man" to "boy."

If you don't remember the correct date or place for a luncheon, call the host and verify. But, if you, for some reason, can't attend and it's too late to postpone or cancel your meeting, call at the earliest moment, apologize and reschedule...if possible.

Keep It Simple...Keep It small

Today's business professional is faced with juggling a tremendous number of responsibilities into very short time frame. Because of these demands, most professionals tend to eat quickly...usually at warp-speed. In a business mealtime situation, if you know you are a slow eater, don't order a large portion. Some prefer to order a salad only or a plate of appetizers, just to keep up with the pace of the "regulars" at the table.

Said one corporate executive, "I never eat more than a salad—because it's better than eating a heavy meal, healthwise, and if I'm not focused totally on food, I am more effective in negotiating, building relationships or whatever the goals of the meal. Bottom-line, I feel more in control."

Power Breakfasts

◆

The Power Breakfast: A Perfect Setting for Urgent Agendas

◆

Business breakfasts have been going on for ages. What's new in the '90s is the "power breakfast," a one-hour, let's-get-down-to-business-immediately session to review an event happening later that day or to meet with people who don't normally do lunch.

The important question to be asked when planning any breakfast meeting is: "Does the reason we're meeting merit me asking another person to wake up an hour earlier?" If you cannot answer with a resounding "yes," the power breakfast may not be the best idea.

And, some business professionals are using "tea" as a new power meal. This brief break in the afternoon is ideal for getting to know someone better. Those who've tried "power teas" say they are a better alternative than breaking up the day with lunch and it also doesn't involve any alcoholic beverages.

Surviving the Business Buffet

◆

Surviving the Business Buffet

◆

First, have a plan: Once again, many folks view a reception or buffet—like any business event where the corporation is picking up the tab—as a "free for all." And it may be. But for you, the candidate, this isn't the time or place to catch up on your calories or your Coronas.

When invited to a business buffet, first do your homework. Decide on your personal goals for attending—like meeting the company's management team, meeting more people who work for the company that is wooing you for a position or perhaps your goal is just getting a look at the group where you could possibly be working.

When To Arrive: If the invitation says the reception is 6:30 p.m. to 8:30 p.m., don't show up at 6:15—very impolite. Come anytime between 6:30 and 8:30 p.m. That's what the invitation said—"any time" between 6:30 p.m. and 8:30 p.m. This isn't rocket science! But ask, if possible, to confirm.

Arrive With a Purpose: So, with purpose in mind, arrive at the appointed hour—and keep a positive outlook. Walk in with a purpose. Some people sort of "ooze" into a room. Be sure you don't do this. Avoid "oozing" anywhere, anytime.

Remember, first impressions are lasting. Have your shoes polished, your suit well-fitted and a smile on your face to project a positive attitude.

Also, if you have a cell phone, leave it in the car during important business luncheons and buffets. A cell phone is not only distracting, but is often viewed as an obnoxious intrusion. The same can be said for the person constantly checking their pager or leaving the room for calls.

First Meet the People, Then Get Your Food: Yes, there's a buffet and a bar on site, but your purpose is meeting people, making connections and getting into conversations, so the food and the drinks can wait.

If there are nametags fill one out by printing your first and last names—large and legibly. Then place your nametag on the right shoulder.

When you extend your right hand to introduce yourself, the other's person's gaze will naturally fall to your right shoulder.

Women should shake hands firmly with each other, and also with men. Both a women and man may initiate a business handshake, which should be a solid, firm grip. It is a sign of weakness for a woman to offer bent, princess-like fingers instead of a full hand.

Men should not try to show their prowess by the strength of their grip, a simply, full-bodied handshake will do.

Remember, too, when shaking hands with someone for the first time, make eye contact first with their faces and then take a look at their nametag. It will help you remember their name later.

Keep the conversation clean, the jokes clever or to yourself and this is not the place for either sexual innuendoes in your conversation or excessive flirting.

Going Through the Buffet: When it's time to visit the buffet, just take a little of each thing. Don't load your plate like you haven't eaten in days. Why? Because if you carry this loaded plate as you visit with the hosts and other prospective peers, they will see your piggy portions and this will create a negative impression.

NEVER TAKE BITES WHILE FILLING YOUR PLATE AT THE BUFFET TABLE.

As with any business setting where alcohol is served, this isn't the place to over-drink. Take one or two cocktails and then switch to sparkling water or cola.

Don't eat and drink at the same time. If you are standing, hold your drink in your left hand so your right hand is free for shaking in introductions. This way, it won't be wet and chilled from holding the glass. Always keep one hand available for a handshake.

If you visit the buffet table and napkins are provided instead of serving plates, carefully keep track of the toothpicks from the tidbits and throw them away with your napkin. Never deposit toothpicks in a potted plant or on the floor. The same goes for olive pits and shrimp tails. Never put them in the potted plant or in your pocket.

Taste Test Before Taking a Big Bite: If you think something is spicy hot, test it with the tip of your tongue before taking a bite. This approach may help you avoid an embarrassing scene. And, if you happen to find something hotter than you can handle—or something that tastes bad—don't spit it out immediately. Turn your head and transfer it into a napkin and then find a wastebasket and dispose of the napkin there. Don't leave it on your plate or wadded on the table.

And one more reminder about buffet food: If there is dip, NEVER dip anything you've already taken a bite from—like chips or veggies.

If you see someone you know, it's almost a relief to see a familiar face. Greet them and enjoy a brief conversation, but make certain you circulate. And after you've met another group and chatted for a while, excuse yourself to get another bite from the buffet table or another drink and move to the next group.

When Spouses or Significant Others Go Along: First of all, make certain spouses, etc., are invited. Don't just show up with yours in tow. Some executives get miffed when they have a business affair and end up paying a double price tag because people have brought their friends or spouses along.

If spouses or friends are invited and your (husband or wife or significant other) doesn't mingle well, it is permissible leave them at home and make an excuse about them being otherwise engaged. If they do want to accompany you, don't leave them sitting over in a corner while you work the room. Bring them along, introduce them and then continue conversation—and don't spend too much time with any one group.

At the end of the evening—and you should plan your departure before the ending time stated on the invitation—make it a point to find the host or one of their representatives. Thank them for a nice evening, the sumptuous buffet and for including you. Then, quietly make your departure.

The Mandatory Thank-you: And, as with any business meeting or social occasion, a thank-you note is not just necessary. It's a requirement for the savvy professional who expects to advance and succeed.

It's About Relationships— and Knowing Which Fork To Use!

It's a known fact—people will draw conclusions about you and the way you conduct yourself at this lunch. They, then, take these conclusions and apply them to how you would fit in the office situation. That's why it is important to dress conservatively, wear a conservative hairstyle, and be well groomed—and understated—at the luncheon.

Be conversant but don't be too "talkie." Be pleasant but don't gush. Be open but not transparent. Be positive but not hyper.

We are not all born with these innate social skills. For many of us, it is a matter of practice and more practice until we feel at ease. So, we'll suggest you take every luncheon invitation and use it as a classroom where you are learning new skills and developing the ones you already have. And while you're there, observe others and how they conduct themselves.

Remember too…no experience is ever wasted, no matter how fulfilling or how painful. Learn from them all!

Conclusions

◆

Conclusions

$\blacklozenge$

"60 Minutes To Success" was written as a tool for members of the American workforce as they continue the journey toward ultimate career goals, success and self-fulfillment.

Be advised. There are no magic formulas, no tried-and-true methods. Getting the job you want may not happen your first time out. For some, it takes years of "paying dues" to finally land in the job of their dreams.

In the meantime, be prepared, be equipped, be polished in your presentation and, most important of all, be yourself with all you have to offer.

A veteran recruiter once said, "We tire of hearing questions about what being with our company will do for the candidates. It's always so refreshing to hear a candidate let us know what they can—and want—to do for our company. That kind of attitude gets my attention every time."

Recruiters' Most Memorable Tales

◆

Recruiters' Most Memorable Tales

◆

On the Wild Side—Think You've Heard Everything?

From a column by Bob Levy in "The Washington Post:"

One candidate chewed bubble gum and constantly blew bubbles. Another candidate said if he were hired, he'd get a tattoo of the corporate emblem to demonstrate his loyalty.

And another rare candidate—took off a shoe and sock, sprinkled medicated powered on his foot and in his shoe. By way of explanation, he said he had to use the powder four times a day and now was one of those times.

From Sherry Mader, Western Wisconsin Technical College: A top accounting student interviewed for a prized position and was not accepted. When the career services officer inquired as to why the student didn't get the job, the interviewer said that her fingernails were not well groomed and he would not hire anyone to do accounting who did not pay attention to details.

From Barry L. O'Donnell, Virginia Tech: One of our MBA students went to Chapel Hill as an undergrad and was invited for an interview with a company in that area. Her mother decided she needed a new interview suit, so they went shopping, selected the appropriate suit and left it to be altered. The next week, just before the interview, the candidate returned to pick up the suit, took it home and started to dress for her appointment.

Nobody knows how she got out of the store without detection, but when she took the skirt off the hanger, she noticed it still had the plastic security tag attached. Knowing it would require a return trip to the store to have the tag removed, the candidate tried on the jacket but found it didn't cover the tag. Luckily, her mother had a jacket of a similar color that was a longer cut...long enough to hide the security tag.

The interview went well and the candidate was taken on a tour of the computer facility by her prospective employer. As they passed through the security frame, the alarm sounded. The prospective boss tried to pass it off by saying, "These darn things get screwed up sometimes. Are you wearing any metal?"

"Nope," responded the candidate.

"Let's try it again."

And again the alarm sounded...Buzz-z-z-z!

Of course, the candidate was not about to tell him about the security tag on her new skirt, fearful that he would think she had shop-lifted the garment.

The boss says not to worry, takes her through the computer center and later offers her the job.

The candidate accepts the position and performs well for more than a year before deciding to return to school for her MBA.

Her last day on the job, her boss takes her out to lunch and she confesses: "Remember when the alarms went off during my interview tour?" she queried.

Boss: "Yet—never figured that out. We had the vendor technician tear that thing down to the last bolt and could never figure out what was wrong."

The candidate told her story, the boss was appropriately amused by her dilemma...and to this day, whenever they meet, he greets her by saying "Buzz-z-z."

From Kathy Woughter, Alfred University (NY): One interviewer who came to campus once asked to bring a Polaroid camera to photograph all his interviewees. He said it would make the candidates easier to remember. His request was declined, but later—during an evaluation—said cameras should be provided for the same purpose.

From Robert Fuller, Director of Career Services, Briar Cliff College (IA): Recruiters from 100 of the nation's largest corporations described their most unusual experiences—One job applicant challenged the interviewer to an arm wrestle while another applicant wore a Walkman, explaining she could listen to the interviewer and the music at the same time. One candidate came to the interview with a paper bag, announced that she hadn't had lunch and proceeded to eat a burger and fries in the interviewer's office. And then there was the candidate who said he never finished high school because he was kidnapped and kept in a closet in Mexico.

The same group was asked to remember their most unusual questions: "Do I have to dress for the next interview? What is it you people do in this company? Will the company move my rock collection from California to Maryland? Does your company have a policy regarding concealed weapons?"

And the recruiters were also asked to contribute some of the most unusual statements made by candidates: "Sometimes I feel like smashing things. Women should not be allowed to drink in cocktail bars. Almost everyone is guilty of bad sexual conduct. I never get hungry. If the pay were right, I'd travel with the carnival. My legs are really hairy...and, I think I'm going to throw up."

Related Readings

———————— ◆ ————————

"A Funny Thing Happened at the Interview" by Gregory A. Farrell (Edin Books, Inc.)

"At Ease Professionally" by Hilka Klinkenberg.

"Business Etiquette and Professionalism: Your Guide to Career Success" by M. Kay DuPonte (Crisp Publications—1990).

"Business Etiquette in Brief: The Competitive Edge for Today's Professional" by Ann Marie Sabath (Bob Adams—1993).

"Dress Casually for Success…for Men." (McGraw-Hill—1997).

"Emily Post on Business Etiquette" by Elizabeth L. Post (HarperPerennial—1990)

"Executive Etiquette in the New workplace. An Indispensable Guide to the Corporate Conduct That Will Launch and Develop Anyone's Career" by Marjabelle Young Stewart and Marian Faux (St. Martin's Griffin—1996)

"Gaining the Competitive Edge with Business Etiquette: How to Avoid the Ten Most Common Faux Pas" (videotape by At East—1989).

"Job Interviews for Dummies" by Joyce Lain Kennedy

"Miss Manners' Guide to Excruciatingly Correct Behavior" by Judith Martin (Warner Books)

"The Amy Vanderbilt Compete Book of Etiquette: A Guide to Contemporary Living" by Letitia Baldridge (Doubleday & Co., Inc.—1978).

"Women's Dress for Success" by John T. Molloy (Warner Books—1996).

"VGM's Complete Guide to Career Etiquette: From the Job Search Through Career Advancement" by Mark Satterfield (VGM Career Horizons—1996).

"The Winning Image: Present Yourself with Confidence and Style for Career Success" by James Gray Jr. (American Management Association—1993)

About the Authors

—————————— ◆ ——————————

Alice Adams, M.A. grew up at a table where manners were a high priority. A career journalist, she earned a bachelor's degree in creative writing and a combined master's degree in mass communications and education. She is a candidate for a doctorate in higher education administration at The University of Houston.

Her teaching experience spans more than a decade at the college level, including management courses at Odessa (Texas) College and The University of St. Thomas, Houston. Alice has also been a trainer and curriculum developer for Fortune 500 corporations and has recently developed a total training cycle for an international service firm. Alice and her husband Ron have co-authored several textbooks on communication and management and a handbook on management listening skills with David Cottrell of CornerStone Management.

Alice has been an international lecturer on management topics and has written monthly management columns for several magazines. For the past six years, she has written regularly for The Houston Chronicle, The Jewish Herald-Voice and The Austin American-Statesman. She and her husband live in Austin and are the parents of three sons–Kevin, Erik and Jeffrey.

Ronald T. Adams, Ph.D. is a career educator, working in all phases of teaching and administration in public schools and on the community college level. A graduate of Howard Payne University, he went on to earn a master's degree in mathematics and doctorates in mathematics and exercise physiology from The University of Texas.

As a professional educator and administrator, Ron has authored numerous curricula in age group exercise and health and physical education and has co-authored several textbooks with his wife, Alice. His fitness columns have been published in several newspapers and senior periodicals.

Ron's lifelong interest in fitness has extended from the athletic playing field to the boardroom, where he applies the same principals of preparation, conditioning, the competitive spirit how to gain the winning edge. His hobbies include competition in triathlons and training age group triathletes, travel and xeriscape gardening.

Rachel A. Seff is the former director of the Career Center at the University of Houston College of Business Administration, where she was responsible for the career management of 5,500 undergraduate business majors and MBA candidates. She now directs admissions, recruiting and marketing for Rice University's MBA program. A Yankee by birth and a Texan by choice, Rachel received her undergraduate degree from George Washington University and her master's from Texas A&M University. Rachel is frequently quoted in the national media on issues related to the economy and entry-level hiring.

A community leader, she is active in the Texas A&M alumni organization and has served as a delegate to national conferences on religious, political and social issues.

At the University of Houston, Rachel has organized various training sessions to prepare students for their first formal job searches and serves as a counselor to students from Houston, the U.S. and foreign countries who are seeking to begin their careers with domestic and foreign companies.

Glossary

———◆———

Eastern Restaurant Terms

Daikon Radish—A long sweet tasting radish used prominently in Japanese cooking.

Hijiki—A dried, squiggly black seaweed used in Japanese cooking. Its usually rehydrated before using.

Hoisin Sauce—Also known as Peking sauce. A reddish-brown sweet and spicy Chinese sauce reminiscent of barbecue sauce. It is made from soybeans and peppers and can be found in the Asian section of most grocery stores.

Tahini—An oily paste made from ground sesame seeds.

Tamarind Paste—A vitamin-rich, tangy, prune like pulp from the pods of a tropical Asian tree. It is used as a seasoning in curries and chutneys or made into drinks, jams, or sorbets.

Tofu–Also called bean curd. A soybean curd that comes white cheese like square.

Wasabi—Also called Japanese horseradish, a pungent green paste made from a rhizome of the watercress family.

Kudzu or Kuzu—A Japanese thickener that produces a light, transparent sauce.

French Restaurant Terms

Agneau–Lamb

A la Carte–Each item is priced separately or prepared to order.

A la King–A sauce containing mushrooms, green peppers, and red peppers.

A la Mode–with ice cream. It is usually ice cream served on top of a slice of pie.

Amandine—garnish with almonds.

Au Jus–served with natural juices.

Beurre—Butter

Beurre Manie—Translates to handled butter. It is an equal mixture of soft butter and flour, used for thickening soups and sauces.

Canard–Duck

Chaud—Hot

En Croute—Food baked in a crust.

Gateau–Cake

Gaufres–Wafer

Hor d-oeuvre–appetizers usually served at the beginning of the meal.

Langouste–Crawfish

Noir–Black

Oeuf–Egg

Ragout–Stew

Vert–Green

Viande–Meat

Italian Restaurant Terms

Al Dente—"to the tooth". It refers to the firm but tender consistency a perfectly (in some opinions) cooked piece of pasta will have.

Amaretti—Almond cookies reminiscent of the macaroon.

Amaretto—An almond flavored liqueur (made from apricot pits).

Asiago–A cheese (known as poor man's Parmesan) mainly used for grating.

Carpaccio—Originally, paper thin slices of raw beef with a creamy sauce, invented at Harry's Bar in Venice. In recent years, the term has come to describe very thinly sliced vegeatables, raw or smoked meats, and fish.

Gelato—An Italian ice cream made with a base of milk or egg yolks and milk. It is denser and more icy in texture than American ice creams. It usually has stronger flavors as well.

Gnocchi–dumpling

Gorgonzola—A cow's milk cheese that is white or yellow and streaked with blue. It has a distinct smell and can have a mellow, strong, or sharp flavor, depending on its degree of maturity. It is similar to the American blue cheese and the French roquefort.

Granita—A mixture of water, sugar, and liquid flavorings (i.e. fruit juice or coffee) that is stirred occasionally while being frozen to create a granular texture.

Pancetta–A cured meat made from the belly (pancia) of the big (the same cut used for bacon). It is salted but lightly spiced, but not smoked.

Polenta—A coarse yellow cornmeal mush that is a staple of Northern Italy.

Proscuitto—The Italian word for ham, used in the names of raw hams coming from Italy.

Zabaglione—A custard like dessert made solely of egg yolks, sugar, and (traditionally) Marsala wine.

Spanish and Mexican

Arroz Con Pollo—rice with chicken.

Capon—A young, neutered rooster, ranging in size from 4 to 10 pounds.

Chipotle—Smoked dried jalapeno chiles. The distinctive smoky heat of chipotles is used to flavor Southwestern and Mexican dishes.

Chorizo—A highly spiced, coarsely ground pork sausage.

Crema Mexicana—A cream that has the same amount or more of butterfat as whipping cream similar to creme fraiche.

Crema Fresca Casera–Translated "homestyle fresh cream".

Crema Centroamerica—A cream that is as rich as whipping cream like mascarpone.

Creme de Casis—A sweet cordial flavored with black currants.
Enchiladas—are softened tortillas that are filled and rolled usually covered with a sauce.

Jocoque—A Mexican style sour cream.

Masa Harina—Corn dough used mainly for tortillas and tamales.

Mole—is a spicy, rich sauce consisting of nuts, seeds, spices, chocolate, and peppers.

Pico de Gallo—a coarse uncooked tomato salsa.

Salsa–a dip for tortilla chips that is made of chopped tomatoes, onions, peppers, and limes. It can be spicy or mild.

Sopapillas–a fried dessert tortilla sprinkled with cinnamon and sugar or honey.

Tacos—are fried tortillas filled with meat or beans.

Tomatillos—Small, green, firm, tomatoescovered with a husk.

Tortillas—Mexican pancakes that are either made of flour or *masa harina.*